C000009486

MATH ON MY PATH

Math at the MARKET

1 → orange

2

3

green

red

5

Rourke Educational Media

A Division of Carson Dellosa Education

Elise Craver

BEFORE AND DURING READING ACTIVITIES

Before Reading: *Building Background Knowledge and Vocabulary*

Building background knowledge can help children process new information and build upon what they already know. Before reading a book, it is important to tap into what children already know about the topic. This will help them develop their vocabulary and increase their reading comprehension.

Questions and Activities to Build Background Knowledge:

1. Look at the front cover of the book and read the title. What do you think this book will be about?
2. What do you already know about this topic?
3. Take a book walk and skim the pages. Look at the table of contents, photographs, captions, and bold words. Did these text features give you any information or predictions about what you will read in this book?

Vocabulary: *Vocabulary Is Key to Reading Comprehension*

Use the following directions to prompt a conversation about each word.
- Read the vocabulary words.
- What comes to mind when you see each word?
- What do you think each word means?

> **Vocabulary Words:**
> - columns
> - equal
> - estimate
> - weigh

During Reading: *Reading for Meaning and Understanding*

To achieve deep comprehension of a book, children are encouraged to use close reading strategies. During reading, it is important to have children stop and make connections. These connections result in deeper analysis and understanding of a book.

 ### Close Reading a Text

During reading, have children stop and talk about the following:
- Any confusing parts
- Any unknown words
- Text to text, text to self, text to world connections
- The main idea in each chapter or heading

Encourage children to use context clues to determine the meaning of any unknown words. These strategies will help children learn to analyze the text more thoroughly as they read.

When you are finished reading this book, turn to the last page for an **After Reading Activity**.

Table of Contents

Math Is All Around

Have you ever gone shopping at the market or grocery store? Each aisle is full of math!

There are things to count.

There are things to measure.

What math do you see?

5

Numbers at the Market

Look at the cookies. How can you put them in groups?

How many do you think are in each group?

Take a guess!

What do you **estimate** is the total number of cookies?

These tomatoes grew in a line.

It can make them easier to count.

These bananas are sold in a group.

How would you count two groups of bananas?

These donuts are placed in rows and **columns.** How does that help you find how many?

These eggs are grouped equally too.
How many are in each group?

What other ways can you put the eggs in **equal** groups?

11

Measuring at the Market

Think about picking up a watermelon. How heavy does it feel?

Think about picking up an apple.
How heavy does it feel?

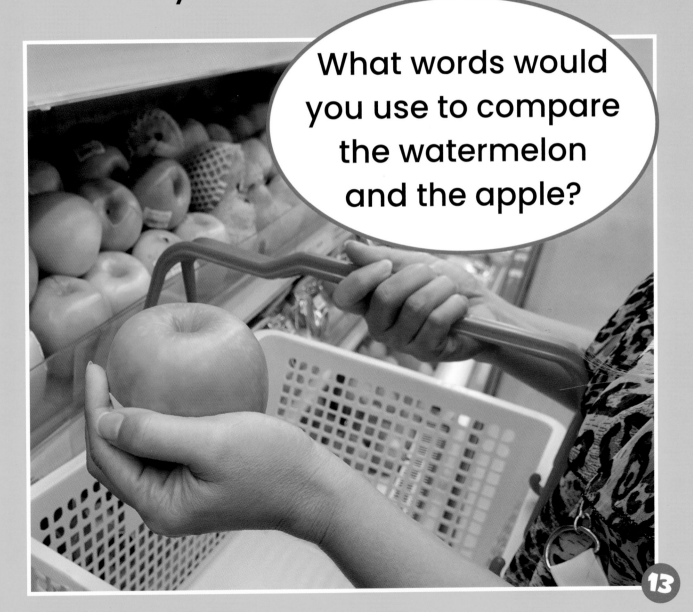

What words would you use to compare the watermelon and the apple?

13

You can use a scale to **weigh** fruits and vegetables.

How much do you think these oranges weigh?

If we add one more orange, what will happen?

Take a peek in the bakery. There are so many types of bread!

What words could you use to compare the different types of bread?

Shapes at the Market

Yum, fresh pizza!

What shapes do you see?

Many fruits are spheres. Can you name another fruit that is like a sphere?

Look at all of the peanut butter jars!
How are they like cylinders?

How are they different?

This can is a cylinder.

What other shapes would you find at the market?

21

Photo Glossary

columns (KAH-luhmz): Sets of things arranged in up-and-down lines.

equal (EE-kwuhl): The same as something else in size or amount.

about 10 orange

estimate (ES-tuh-mate): To use what you know to make a smart guess about how many or how much.

weigh (way): To measure how heavy something is using units such as ounces, pounds, grams, or kilograms.

Activity: I Spy Shapes

What shapes do you see at the market? Make an
I Spy book featuring your finds!

Supplies

construction paper

printer paper

hole punch

yarn

pen or marker

grocery store ads (online or from the mail)

scissors

glue

Directions

1. Use sheets of construction paper for the front and back covers. Add five to ten sheets of printer paper in between for the book pages. Hole punch the left side and tie yarn through the holes to bind the book.

2. Label the top of each page with a shape you are looking for. Include both 2-D and 3-D shapes! You may need to divide each page in half and place two shapes on a page, depending on how many pages are in your book.

3. Decorate the cover. Give it a title such as "I Spy Shapes."

4. Look through grocery store ads on the computer or from the mail. Print or cut out any items you see that match a shape in your book. Glue them to the correct page in your book. Were there shapes you found a lot of? Very few of? Compare the items you see for each shape—how are they the same? Different?

Index

About the Author

Elise Craver is a former teacher who lives in North Carolina and loves to visit the local farmer's market. She didn't like math as a kid but loves it now. She and her two kids are always looking for math problems in real life.

After Reading Activity

There is a lot more math at the market! Think about a time you visited a store or looked at an advertisement. What kinds of math did you see in the prices and sales? Talk about it with your family or a friend.

Library of Congress PCN Data

Math at the Market / Elise Craver
(Math on My Path)
ISBN 978-1-73163-836-6 (hard cover)(alk. paper)
ISBN 978-1-73163-913-4 (soft cover)
ISBN 978-1-73163-990-5 (e-Book)
ISBN 978-1-73164-067-3 (ePub)
Library of Congress Control Number: 2020930049

Rourke Educational Media
Printed in the United States of America
01-1942011937

Edited by: Hailey Scragg
Cover design by: Rhea Magaro-Wallace, Lynne Schwaner
Interior design by: Kathy Walsh, Alison Tracey
Photo Credits: Cover, p 1 ©gece33; p 5 ©Hispanolistic; p 6, 7, 22 ©SamuelBrownNG; p 8 ©fotosipsak; p 9 ©Natissima; p 10, 22 ©LindasPhotography; p 11, 22 ©Brasil2; p 12 ©Evgenii Motroshin; p 13 ©Sasithorn Phuapankasemsuk; p 14 ©anna1311; p 15, 22 ©FangXiaNuo; p 16 ©serezniy; p 17 ©WDnet; p 18 ©HDesert; p 19 ©Jasonfang; p 20 ©toddmedia; p 21 XiXinXing